WHY DO WOLVES HOWL?

Questions and Answers About Wolves

BY MELVIN AND GILDA BERGER
ILLUSTRATED BY ROBERTO OSTI

CONTENTS

KEY TO ABBREVIATIONS

cm = centimeter/centimetre
cm^2 = square centimeter/centimetre
ha = hectare
kg = kilogram
km = kilometer/kilometre
km^2 = square kilometer/kilometre
kph = kilometers/kilometres per hour
m = meter/metre

Text copyright © 2001 by Melvin and Gilda Berger
Illustrations copyright © 2001 by Roberto Osti
All rights reserved. Published by Scholastic Inc.
SCHOLASTIC and associated logos are trademarks and/or registered trademarks of
Scholastic Inc.

No part of this publication may be reproduced, or stored in a retrieval system, or
transmitted in any form or by any means, electronic, mechanical, photocopying,
recording, or otherwise, without written permission of the publisher. For information
regarding permission, write to Scholastic Inc., Attention: Permissions Department,
555 Broadway, New York, NY 10012.

ISBN 0-439-19379-6

Book design by David Saylor and Nancy Sabato

10 9 8 7 6 5 4 3 2 1   01 02 03 04 05

Printed in the U.S.A   08
First printing, January 2001

Expert reader: Don Moore
Curator of Animals
Wildlife Conservation Society
Central Park Wildlife Center
New York, NY

The wolves on the front cover and title page are gray wolves.

For Zach and Val, with all best wishes
— M. AND G. BERGER

To my family
— R. OSTI

INTRODUCTION

If you lived 100 years ago, you would have seen many more wolves than you can see today. Experts estimate there were millions of wolves just a few generations ago. Today, there are only about 200,000 wolves left in the entire world. What happened to the wolves?

Over the years, people settled in places where the wolves lived and hunted. The settlers turned the woods and fields into farms and ranches. They shot many wolves and their prey.

As a result, the wolves that were left found fewer wild animals to hunt. They began to prey on ranchers' sheep and cattle because they did not have enough to eat. They raided farmers' coops and fed on their chickens.

Of course, this made the ranchers and farmers very angry. They shot, trapped, and poisoned the wolves. The number of wolves decreased dramatically. Almost everywhere, wolves were in danger of disappearing forever.

Recently, things began to change. People discovered that wolves are vital to the balance of life in the wild. Governments and scientists are trying to save the wolves.

Now, the wolves are slowly increasing in numbers. Year by year, you can hear their howls—AH-WOOOO—ring out in more and more places. What a thrilling sound!

Melvin Berger   Gilda Berger

WILD AND WONDERFUL

Why do wolves howl?

To send messages. Wolves howl to bring pack members together before a hunt. They howl to locate other wolves and help them find their way back to the pack. They howl to scare away enemies and to warn others of danger. They howl when their bellies are full. And sometimes they seem to howl just for the fun of it!

A wolf researcher once tried howling like a wolf. Some wolves heard his howl from 4 miles (6.4 km) away—and howled back!

When do wolves howl?

Any time of the day or night. Wolves have been heard howling in the morning, afternoon, and evening—and during all seasons of the year.

But the most exciting howling often comes before a hunt. On a calm night, the sounds can carry a very long distance. They can be heard over an area of about 120 square miles (310.8 km²)!

Do wolves howl at the moon?

No, it may just look that way. When wolves howl, they usually point their muzzles upward and forward toward the sky. This makes it seem as if the wolves are howling at the moon. But they're not!

You may think that wolves only howl standing up. But that's not so, either. Wolves can howl from any position—standing, sitting on their haunches, or even lying down.

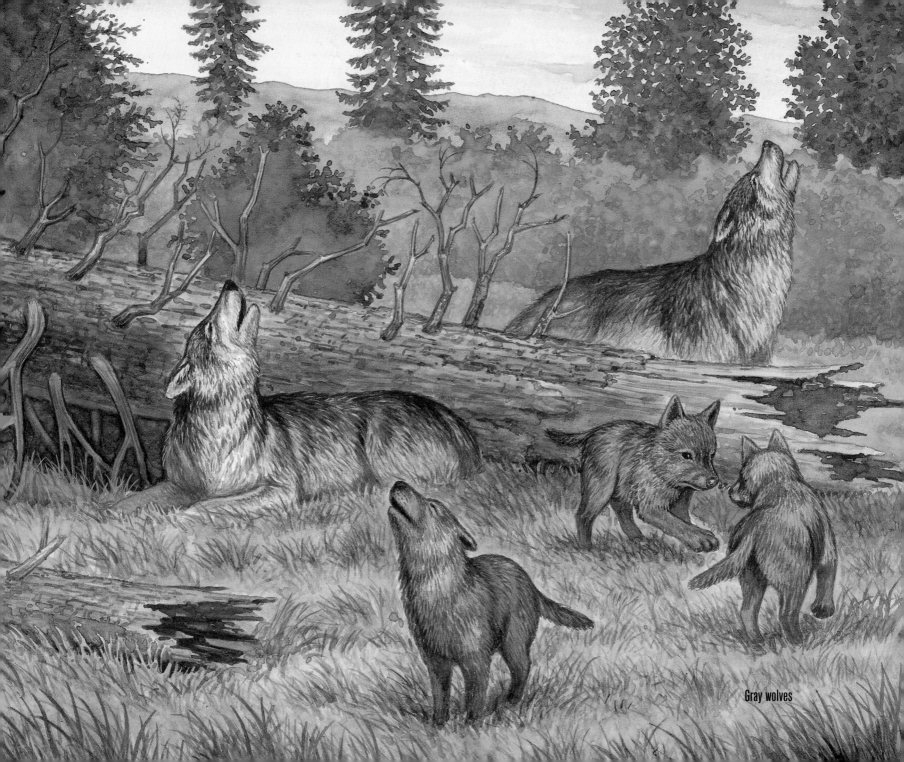

Gray wolves

Giant ground sloth

Prehistoric wolves

When did wolves first appear on Earth?

About one or two million years ago. The early wolves differed from today's wolves in a few ways. For one thing, they had bigger brains, which means they were probably more intelligent. Also, their jaws were longer. But all in all, they looked much like the wolves of today.

Are wolves related to dogs?

Yes. About 10,000 years ago, people began to tame wolves. Some wolves stood out from the rest. They varied slightly in color, size, strength, body and head shape, hair length, or personality.

Over many, many generations, people mated certain wolves for their special features. Eventually, they became the animals that we call dogs.

Today, there are dogs of many sizes, shapes, and colors. But one thing is certain: All dogs are descended from wolves.

Which dog looks most like a wolf?

The German shepherd. But there are some differences. The wolf has longer legs, bigger feet, thicker hair, and weighs more.

Dogs and wolves belong to the same large group, or genus, known as *Canis*. The word itself means "dog." Besides wolves and dogs, *Canis* also includes jackals and dingoes.

Wolves are the largest animals in the dog family, or *Canidae*. Like German shepherds and all other dogs, wolves are social, smart, playful, and loyal.

Are all wolves alike?

No. There are about 20 different kinds of wolves. Among them are the Mexican wolf, Hudson Bay wolf, Rocky Mountain wolf, Texas gray wolf, Great Plains wolf, and Greenland wolf.

Scientists who study wolves often tell them apart by their size and fur. Some wolves are larger and more powerful than others. Some have thicker, longer fur. Wolves vary in color, from pure white to solid black. But every wolf, except the red wolf and the Abyssinian wolf, belongs to the same species, which scientists call *Canis lupus* ("wolf dog").

How large are wolves?

They vary in size. From snout to tail, most wolves range from 40 inches (100 cm) long, the size of a German shepherd, to 63 inches (160 cm) long, as big as a Saint Bernard. The smallest wolf in the world is the Arabian wolf. Its body is only 32 inches (81.3 cm) long.

One male wolf from Alaska set the record for weight. It tipped the scale at 175 pounds (79.3 kg)—the weight of a full-grown man!

Arabian wolf

Where do wolves live?

Almost everywhere except tropical rain forests and arid deserts. Some scientists consider wolves among the most adaptable of animals. Wolves live on the arctic tundra, plains or steppes, grasslands, swamps, mountain ranges, and forests.

German shepherd

Gray wolf

Are wolves good hunters?

Yes, indeed. Wolves are among the most successful of all hunting animals. In areas where they live, wolves are the top predators in the food chains. That means that wolves eat other animals, called prey, but almost no other animal eats them.

As top predators, wolves play a special role in the environment. By trimming the size of animal herds, they help keep a balance between the different plants and animals in their territory.

What animals do wolves hunt?

Any animal that they can catch. But the wolves' main prey are moose, deer, elk, caribou, and bison—all animals much larger than themselves. Among them, moose and bison are the most dangerous prey because of their great size and strength.

Wolves also eat smaller animals, such as beavers, rabbits, mice, and squirrels. In fact, wolves are among the least fussy of all meat eaters!

How do wolves attack their prey?

With their powerful jaws and 42 teeth. Wolves bite with a force of 1,500 pounds (680.4 kg) per square inch (6.45 cm^2). That's about twice the strength of a dog's jaws!

A wolf's teeth are like the teeth of a dog—except that they are bigger and stronger. The four long, pointed canine teeth, or fangs, in front can be 2 inches (5.1 cm) long. They can grab and hold a moose or other prey.

Farther back in the jaw are larger teeth. They have other jobs to do. The sharp teeth along the sides cut through tough flesh; the flat back teeth crush bones. The small teeth in front pick meat off the bones. When wolves are done eating, there's not much left to gnaw on!

Do wolves chew their food?

No. Wolves' teeth are not fit for chewing. Instead, the animals rip large chunks of meat from their prey and swallow them whole.

Scientists examined one wolf's stomach. They found a caribou's ear, tongue, lip, kidneys, liver, windpipe, and large bites of caribou flesh. Quite a meal!

Gray wolf

Bison

Wolf jaws and teeth

How do wolves walk?

On their toes, not on the soles of their feet. This lengthens their legs. Like stilts, long legs let wolves take longer steps.

Long legs also allow wolves to leap through thick layers of snow. While chasing prey, wolves can bound as far as 16 feet (4.9 m) to clear a giant snowdrift. A scientist once tracked a pair of wolves plowing through 6-foot-deep (1.8 m) fluffy snow for 22 miles (35.3 km)!

Are wolves good runners?

Yes. Strong muscles and long legs let wolves run for hours without getting tired.

Wolves' legs are spaced close together. On each side, the hind foot steps in the track made by the front foot. This is very helpful when running in snowy country or over rough ground.

You can always tell a wolf's tracks in the snow. They form one neat line.

What is a wolf's top speed?

About 40 miles an hour (64 kph). But wolves only run this fast when pursuing prey. Usually they trot along more slowly, which is called loping.

Which is a wolf's strongest sense?

Smell. Some say a wolf can smell odors about 100 times better than a human can. A wolf's sense cells cover an area the size of a large handkerchief. In humans, the sense-cell area is only as big as a postage stamp.

Experts tell us that wolves mainly use smell to find their large prey. With their sensitive noses, wolves can pick up the scent of a deer from more than 1 mile (1.6 km) away!

Gray wolf

Do wolves have good hearing?

Yes. In a forest, wolves can hear a howl from as far away as 10 miles (16 km).

When wolves stand still, they keep their ears up. Turning their ears from side to side helps them locate sound.

Scientists believe wolves locate small prey mostly by sound.

Do wolves have good eyesight?

Not especially. Wolves often smell or hear things long before they see them.

But wolves' eyes are sharp in one way. They're quick to spot moving objects—a valuable trait in hunting animals!

Gray wolf

What is the most common kind of wolf?

The gray wolf. Gray wolves can be any color from white to black—although most are gray. Often, their fur is a mixture of shades, including gold, tan, brown, and rust. Darker fur usually runs along the center of the back and tail—except in very old wolves, which tend to be grayer than younger ones.

What are timber wolves?

Dark-colored gray wolves. Timber wolves have pointed ears and short-haired fur. They usually live in heavy forests. Their dark, furry coats make them hard to see among the trees.

Timber wolf

What are tundra or arctic wolves?

Gray wolves with light or white fur. You can tell tundra wolves by their small, rounded ears and longer hair. Tundra wolves live in very snowy areas. Their small ears help conserve body heat in the cold. And their long, thick, white, furry coats keep them warm and provide good camouflage in the snow.

Tundra wolf

Arctic hare

Which wolves look like foxes?

Red wolves. Smaller than most other wolves, red wolves look more like very large foxes than gray wolves.

The fur of the red wolf is not actually red. The usual color is a blend of reddish-brown, black, and gray-brown.

Red wolves once roamed the fields and forests of the southern United States in great numbers. At last count, however, there were only about 80 left in the wild.

Red wolf

What are Mexican wolves?

Wolves that live in the southwestern United States and northern Mexico. Mexican wolves are the smallest wolves in North America. They hunt rabbits and other small animals in the deserts that are their natural habitat.

By 1942, government scientists declared the Mexican wolf extinct in the wild. Since then, they have been working to bring these wolves back. The scientists breed the wolves in zoos and release them into the wild. Today, there are only about 200 Mexican wolves. Most are in captivity.

Mexican wolf

PACKS AND FAMILIES

What is a wolf pack?

A group of as many as 12 wolves that stay together. The pack resembles a large human family. It usually includes a mother and a father, their offspring, and sometimes a few other adults—uncles and aunts. As humans do, the members share and care for one another.

Do most wolves travel alone or in packs?

In packs. Most wolves are friendly, social animals that generally roam and rest in packs. Members bring one another food, play together, help parents raise their young—and even baby-sit for them.

When hunting, pack members cooperate. As you know, wolves can kill animals much larger than themselves. It's surely safer and easier when the pack does the job together.

Who leads the pack?

Usually a male wolf, the largest and strongest in the group. He is called the alpha male. (Alpha is the first letter of the Greek alphabet.)

A wolf pack usually starts when an alpha male and an alpha female pair up. They are the pack leaders. When it's time to hunt, the alpha male gathers the pack together and leads the way.

Alpha gray wolf

Alpha gray wolf

Pack gray wolf

What happens when an alpha wolf and a pack wolf quarrel?

The two wolves growl at each other. They bare their teeth. It looks as if each is about to attack.

But the alpha wolf quickly shows its rank. It stands tall and raises its head. Its ears move forward and point up. It holds its tail high in the air. And it glares at the other wolf.

Usually the pack wolf backs down. It cowers with a lowered tail and flattened ears. Sometimes it tucks its tail between its legs or rolls onto its back to show that it gives up.

The quarrel is over. Neither wolf is hurt. The alpha wolf trots away—head, ears, and tail held high. Pack members may quarrel, but fights are soon forgotten.

What is a lone wolf?

A male or female wolf that lives and hunts by itself. A lone wolf can't kill big animals. So it mostly hunts small prey, such as mice, rabbits, squirrels, and beavers. In time, the lone wolf may find a mate, have young, and start a pack of its own.

What is a wolf territory?

The area in which a wolf pack lives and hunts. Wolves will drive away strange wolves that stray across the boundaries of their territory.

The size of a territory varies. Where there is plenty of game, the territory may be no more than 25 square miles (64.7 km²) in size. But in areas where there is little prey, the territory may stretch out over 5,000 square miles (13,000 km²).

How do wolves mark their territory?

With urine. The wolves mark rocks, stumps, logs, ice chunks, or sticks with their own scent.

Wolves can tell the scents of pack members from those of strangers. Simply smelling the scent mark lets wolves know whether they are in their own territory or that of another pack. From time to time, the wolves will renew the scent marks—just to be sure that everyone knows the boundaries.

How do wolves show their feelings?

Mostly with their faces. In general, bared teeth and ears straight up show anger. When a wolf is afraid, it may flatten its ears against its head and let its tongue hang out. A suspicious wolf pulls its ears back and narrows its eyes.

A wolf's tail also expresses feelings. A wolf threatening another raises its tail. A frightened animal holds its tail very low, often tucked in between its legs or curled forward alongside its legs. And a wolf freely wagging its tail signals happiness, just as it does in a dog.

How do wolves "talk" to each other?

By howling and making other sounds. Growling is an unfriendly sound that wolves make before attacking. Barking is an alarm call or sound of surprise that wolves make when other animals invade their territory. Whining is a noise that adult females produce when they want to show affection or tell the young to stop playing roughly. And soft squeaks seem to say, "Everything's okay."

Who "cries wolf"?

Humans. To "cry wolf" means to call for help when there is no danger.

The expression comes from an old story: A young shepherd yelled for help, again and again. Each time, he claimed that a wolf was attacking his sheep. But it wasn't true. He just wanted to trick the other shepherds. Then, one day, a wolf did attack the shepherd's flock. The young man called for help, but nobody came. Everyone had been fooled too many times before.

Gray wolves

Gray wolves and pups

Does a wolf mate for life?

Probably. A wolf seems to keep the same partner for a very long time. Male and female wolves breed once a year, sometime between late January and April. The exact time depends on where the wolves live.

Where do female wolves give birth?

In dens. Pregnant wolves dig underground burrows, or tunnels, about three weeks before the birth of their pups. The entrance is large enough for the adult wolves to enter easily.

In the spring, the wolf mother, called a dam, goes into the den. She usually gives birth to four, five, or six pups. The pups look like little teddy bears, with short, flat muzzles and a covering of thin gray fur. With eyes closed and ears flopped over, the pups don't leave their mother's side.

Can newborn wolf pups care for themselves?

No. Newborn pups are tiny and helpless. Each one is only 8 inches (20.3 cm) long and weighs about 1 pound (.45 kg). The mother wolf feeds them milk from her body. The male and other pack members bring the mother food to eat.

At about two weeks of age, the pups' eyes open and they begin to stand, walk, and chew. Their muzzles start to grow longer. One more week, and the pups come out of the den. They tumble and wrestle playfully around the entrance.

Why do wolf pups need to play?

To prepare for adult life. Through play, the pups learn which wolves will lead the pack and which ones will follow. Also, the growing pups need to exercise their muscles. Then, when autumn comes, they'll be strong enough to join the adults when they hunt.

When do pups first eat meat?

At about four weeks of age. The pups swarm around an adult who returns from a hunt. The little ones sniff, nibble, and lick the adult's mouth until it coughs up some of the meat it has already eaten. Up comes a meal—right into the hungry pups' mouths. It's their first taste of meat!

At what age do the pups leave the den for the first time?

Three to four weeks. Then, by eight to ten weeks, the pups are ready to live with the rest of the pack. The adults leave the young wolves at resting spots while they hunt. The pups climb, jump, tumble, and roll on the ground with one another. They pounce and fight. They chase insects and small animals. Through play, the young wolves learn to be good hunters.

Female gray wolf and pups

When are pups old enough to kill prey?

At about ten months of age. Before the pups become active hunters, they need to have all their adult teeth. They also must be strong and fast enough to kill large animals. Until then, the young wolves help other pack members run down the prey.

How long do pups hunt with the pack?

For about a year and a half. By then they are full-grown adults. Some stay with the pack. Others leave to find mates and start new packs.

How do wolves find their prey?

Usually by sniffing the air. An alpha wolf notices the smell and points its head in that direction. All the animals stand alert, with their eyes, ears, and noses facing toward the prey. The alpha wolves give the signal—and the pack heads off in that direction.

The pack wolves trot behind the alpha wolf in single file. They make sure the wind is blowing in their faces. This way, they can smell the prey animal, but it cannot smell them.

How do the wolves end the hunt?

With a sudden rush to the prey. When the pack gets close, the wolves spread out. All at once, they charge forward and attack from all sides. One wolf bites the animal's side. Another goes for its hind parts. Others sink their teeth into its neck and nose.

Soon the animal is bleeding from its wounds. It becomes weak and falls to the ground. Eventually, it dies.

Who eats first?

The alpha wolves. The rest wait their turn. Each wolf gulps down as much as 20 pounds (9 kg) of meat at a feeding. But it may not feed again for two weeks!

Do the wolves always bring down their prey?

No. Sometimes the prey fights back. An adult moose can weigh more than 1,000 pounds (450 kg) and be more than 6 feet (2 m) tall at the shoulders. This huge beast can seriously harm the much smaller wolves.

The moose slashes the wolves with its powerful hooves. It butts them with its pointy antlers. The wolves frequently turn and flee.

Other times the prey tries to escape. The wolves give chase. Moose and other large animals can run very fast. They often outrun the wolves. In fact, wolves only catch about 1 out of every 10 moose they hunt!

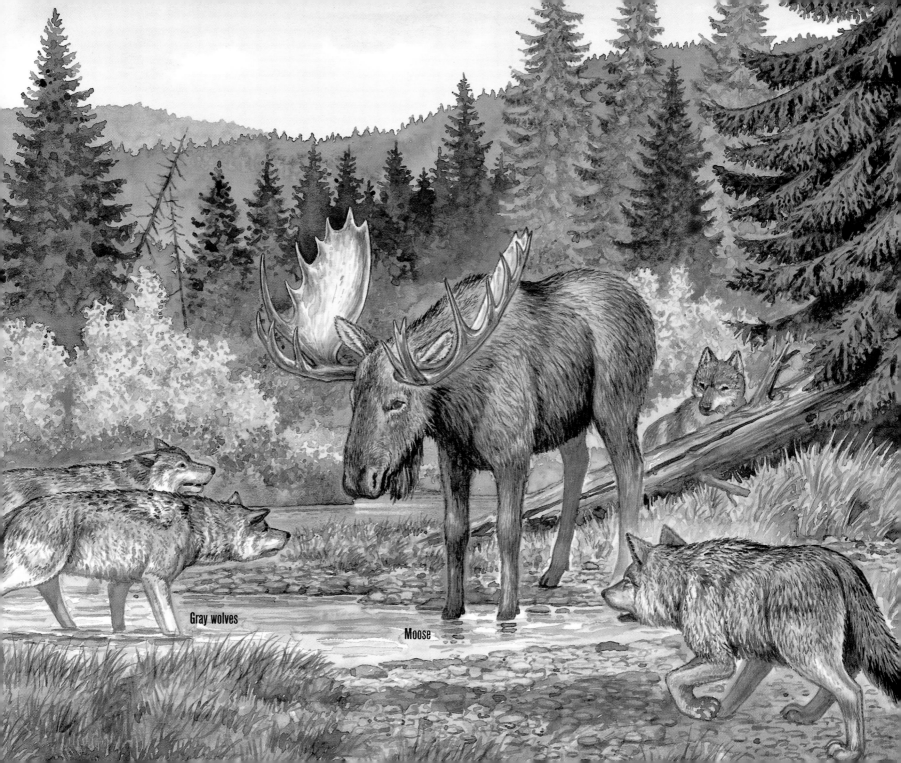

Gray wolves

Moose

Do wolves mostly eat healthy animals?

The very opposite. Wolves find it much easier to hunt sick, injured, and old animals. Seizing weaker animals provides more food for the predator wolves.

When wolves eat sick prey, they keep disease from spreading because they are protected from getting sick themselves. And when wolves make meals of injured or older prey, there is more food for younger, stronger animals.

How long can wolves go without food?

Several days at a time. Wolves probably eat a few times a day when large amounts of food are available. The wolves eat as much as possible each time and digest it quickly. They stay with the prey until all the edible parts are gone.

But when food is not available, wolves seem to be equally well adapted to fasting, or not eating. Scientists think wolves probably can fast for two weeks or longer. The longest a wild wolf is known to have gone without food is 17 days!

Gray wolves

Are wolves night creatures?

Yes and no. During warm seasons, wolves begin to hunt early in the evening and return to the den or resting site by morning. One reason is to conserve energy. It's simply too hot to hunt during the day.

But winter is a different story. Wolves are active day *and* night.

Do wolves migrate?

Some do. Migrating wolves usually live in very cold areas. Here, the ground freezes in the winter. The wolves' prey often head to warmer regions to find food. The wolves follow herds of caribou and other animals to better feeding grounds. They stay there until the spring. Then the wolves follow the herds back to their home territories.

Other wolves live where they can find enough prey animals all winter long. These wolves don't migrate. They stay in the same territory year-round.

How do wolves keep warm in winter?

They grow extra-thick coats of fur. A wolf's coat has two layers. Next to its skin is a soft, dense layer of underfur. A cover of long guard hairs keeps the underfur dry.

In cold weather, wolves tuck their muzzles and noses between their hind legs when they lie down. They cover their faces with their thick, furry tails. And then they sleep, snug and dry.

Gray wolves

WOLVES AND YOU

Are you afraid of wolves?

Many people are. They grow up reading "Little Red Riding Hood" and "The Three Little Pigs." They hear the tale of "Peter and the Wolf." And they believe every myth about the "big, bad wolf."

Many stories about wolves are very, very old. They date back to a time before people understood wolves and their ways. Back then, make-believe took the place of real knowledge about wolves.

Today, we know much more about these wonderful creatures. There's no reason to be afraid of them.

What are werewolves?

Fictional creatures. During the Middle Ages, people believed that some humans changed into wolves at night. They called them werewolves. The idea of werewolves arose from the fear of wolves and the false notion that they are evil and have supernatural powers.

According to this old belief, werewolves ate human flesh and performed horrible deeds. The only way to kill a werewolf was with a silver bullet.

People accused individuals they didn't like of being werewolves. Many innocent men and women were tried, convicted, and executed for the "crime" of being a werewolf. That gives you an idea of how much people feared wolves!

Have wolves ever saved anyone?

In at least one legend. According to an ancient tale, infant twins, Romulus and Remus, were cast into the Tiber River in Italy some 3,000 years ago. The basket that held them drifted to shore. A female wolf found the basket and cared for the babies.

Some years later, a shepherd came upon the twins. He took them home and raised them. In time, they grew to be strong, wise, handsome young men.

More years went by. Romulus decided to found a city on the Tiber River at the spot where he had been found by the wolf. The city was named Rome, after Romulus. It is now the capital city of Italy.

This statue is in the Capitolino Museum in Rome, Italy.

Do wolves attack people?

No. Wolves are generally shy and avoid people if possible.

There are no reports of healthy wolves killing people. In fact, some years ago, a newspaper in Ontario, Canada, offered a reward for any information about a wolf attack on a human. Thus far, no one has come forward to claim the reward.

Do wolves make good pets?

No. Wolves may look like big dogs, but they are still wild animals. Even when raised by humans, they are shy and fearful. Wolves are also hard to train. They belong in the wild, their natural habitat, or protected in zoos.

Do wolves attack farm animals?

Sometimes. Wolves are predators that must have meat to live. Normally, they feed on moose, caribou, and other large wild animals. But sometimes their regular prey is gone, or they come upon sheep and cattle. Then, the wolves follow their natural meat-eating instincts and attack the farm animals.

The state of Minnesota, for example, has more than 325,000 sheep and cattle, and about 1,000 wolves. Due to shortages in their usual prey and the large number of livestock in the state, wolves kill about 500 domestic animals every year.

Do wolves usually kill more animals than they can eat?

No. In the wild, wolves rarely kill more than they need to feed themselves. They eat almost all of a prey animal. All that they leave behind is a pile of bones picked clean of all meat.

But with farm animals, wolves sometimes get confused. The farm animals are often in pens. They are not able to run or defend themselves. Prey are never this easy to catch in nature. The wolves may rip out small chunks of meat and leave the rest of the prey untouched—practically unheard of in the wild!

Do people harm wolves?

Yes. Fear and superstition have led humans to poison, trap, or shoot millions of wolves in many parts of the world.

By the early 1700s, the English had wiped out wolves by hunting or trapping them. People in the rest of western Europe took longer, but also eliminated almost all wolves.

The last wild wolf in Europe was seen in Bainbridge, England, long, long ago. Yet the city still pays someone about $3 a year to scare away the wolves by playing blasts on a buffalo horn! In other places, wolves have survived. There are still between 50,000 and 100,000 wolves in Russia.

When did most wolves disappear from North America?

In the 1800s. People began to settle on the western Great Plains. They killed enormous herds of bison to make room for their ranches and towns.

With their natural prey gone, the wolves preyed on the settlers' animals. To protect their livestock, the settlers started killing the wolves.

How did Americans kill the wolves?

Mostly with poison. Wolf hunters placed poison in the bodies of dead bison, cattle, or sheep. Wolves feeding on the animals died painfully of poisoning. But so did coyotes, dogs, and birds that ate the poisoned flesh. By 1900, there were few wolves left in the western United States. The populations of other wild animals dropped, too.

To make matters worse, the government passed many anti-wolf laws after 1900. Officials offered money, called a bounty, for every dead wolf.

Gray wolves

Tundra wolves in the
Arctic Circle

Do people still kill wolves?

Yes. Farmers and ranchers kill wolves out of fear that the wolves will attack their livestock. Also, hunters kill wolves so manufacturers can use the fur to make coats and rugs and the trim for hoods of jackets.

Business owners, wanting to attract hunters, join those who are eliminating wolves from the countryside. They kill wolves to leave more big game—moose, caribou, and deer—for others to hunt.

Are wolves an endangered species?

Yes. Today, wolves are endangered in all parts of the United States except Minnesota and Alaska. When a kind of animal is put in the endangered species category, it means that the killing of that animal is strictly forbidden.

There are probably fewer than 10,000 wolves in the entire United States. Most of them are in Alaska. In Canada, only about 30,000 wolves remain.

Why does the state of Alaska have the most wolves?

It's the largest state with the fewest people. Much of the state is still wild and natural. Also, about one-third of Alaska is north of the Arctic Circle, home to the tundra, or arctic, wolves.

Can the government help save wolves?

Yes. The Endangered Species Act, passed in 1973, protects most wolves. Government scientists are also working to bring wolves back to wild areas from which they have disappeared.

When did scientists return wolves to Yellowstone National Park?

In 1995 and 1996. Scientists caught 66 wolves in Canada. They captured these animals without harming them in any way. The scientists then flew the wolves to Yellowstone National Park in the United States and placed them in large, 1-acre (0.4 ha), fenced-in pens. The wolves were kept in these pens for just over two months to let them get used to the area. Workers fed them roadkill, large animals that had been accidentally killed by cars. Then, the scientists released the wolves into the wild within the park.

Has this program been successful?

Very. By the beginning of the year 2000, the wolf population in Yellowstone had grown to almost 200. The animals had mated, borne pup litters, and formed a number of separate packs. Experts tell us that the wolves of Yellowstone are here to stay.

How do scientists follow the wolves in Yellowstone?

They track them by radio. Scientists place collars with small radio transmitters on some wolves' necks. They also may implant tiny radios into the wolves' bodies.

As the wolves travel, the radio transmitters send out signals. By following the signals, the scientists can learn about wolves' activities.

Sometimes the scientists attach a tag to a wolf's ear. Each time they see the wolf, they check its tag. This tells the scientists how far the wolf has traveled.

Why do we need wolves?

Because they are vital to life in the wilderness—and wilderness enriches our lives no matter where we live.

Wolves hunt and kill large animals. Many birds and small animals steal bits of meat from the wolves' dinners. Worms and insects feed on the dead animals' remains.

Droppings from all these animals enrich the soil and feed the plants. The growing plants provide food for plant-eating animals. And with plant eaters to prey on, meat-eating animals don't go hungry.

The old saying puts it best: When wolves eat, everyone eats.

Gray wolves

INDEX

About the Authors

The Bergers live in New York, far from the few places in North America where you can still hear the wonderful sound of wolves' howling. Yet, they care deeply about the wilderness and the protection of wildlife and their habitats. "We belong to many wildlife organizations," they say, "and write countless letters to government officials, hoping to improve wildlife laws and practices."

About the Illustrator

Roberto Osti once went to the zoo to see wolves in an enclosed wooded area, but when he looked into the enclosure, he didn't see any wolves! After a while, he felt like he was being observed. Then he noticed a pair of yellow eyes looking at him from a thicket. "Who knows how long the wolf had been watching me!" he says. "Since then, I've been fascinated by these secretive and intelligent animals."